Homemaking
An Invitation To Greatness

Norma Steven
Joyce Orwick

Harvest House Publishers
Irvine, California 92714

All Scripture portions are taken from *The Living Bible*
unless otherwise indicated.

HOMEMAKING, AN INVITATION TO GREATNESS

Copyright © 1978 Harvest House Publishers
Irvine, California 92714
Library of Congress Catalog Card Number: 77-92735
ISBN #0-89081-115-6

Printed in the United States of America.

Homemaking
An Invitation To Greatness

❦❦❦

For Joyce

❦❦❦

Contents

1. YOU'RE THE GREATEST   11
2. A NEW FRIEND   19
3. WALKING WITH THE LORD   25
4. HOUSECLEANING HINTS FOR KITCHEN AND MIND   35
5. GETTING BACK YOUR "OOMPH"   49
6. PRACTICAL THINGS FIRST?   61
7. RESPONSIBLE LIVING   67
8. I'M SHAPING UP   79
9. TRUSTFUL LIVING   85
10. CHILDREN—TO HAVE OR HAVE NOT   95
11. DO WHAT IS BEST FOR YOU   103
12. HOMEMAKING—AN ART AND SCIENCE   115
13. A VACUUM WILL MAKE THE DIFFERENCE   121

14. YOU DON'T KNOW HOW
     RICH YOU ARE   129
15. NEXT YEAR I'LL BE FREE!   141
16. GOOSE BUMPS IN MY STOMACH   147
  EPILOGUE—STEPS TO "GREATNESS"   155

1

You're the
Greatest

1

⚜

Bored. Unfulfilled. Trapped. Who needs it? *I'm* determined *I* will be *myself* first—a woman with my own personal style, and work for my family second.

These words reflect the current feeling of many women—non-Christian and Christian. Unfulfilled in their role as wife and homemaker, many women no longer feel that the "two shall be one," but that the "two shall be two." Conversely, a husband who feels the need for a haven from his work-a-day world, finds he no longer has one and drowns his frustrations in "wine, women, and song," and Monday night football. Children without parental love and guidance, due to parental absence or indifference, get nothing, and as a result, give nothing in return. Commitment is a forgotten word.

But as Christians, Christ calls us to a committed life—to Him and to each other. And this commitment, this being bound to a certain line of conduct, isn't a "maybe," "perhaps," "later on" agreement. We can no longer be the master of our fate. Through what He accomplished for us at Calvary, He is our rightful owner.

We are told throughout Scripture that we who belong to God are to be different. One of these differences found in Matthew 20:25-28 is often overlooked. The mother of James and John wanted her sons to be important to Christ. Her motive was right, but her method was wrong! But Jesus uses this incident to teach an important truth. Important because He best understands our natural drive for greatness (recognition, success).

"Among the heathen," Jesus said, "kings are tyrants and each minor official lords it over those beneath him. But among you it is quite different. Anyone wanting to be a leader among you must be your servant. And if you want to be right at the top, you must serve like a slave. Your attitude must be like my own, for I, the Messiah, did not come to be served, but to serve, and to give my life as a ransom for many."

Do you see why homemaking is an invitation to greatness? There's so many ways to serve! If you dislike the word *serve*, look at it this way: Through your commitment to your rightful responsibilities, you can render spiritual obedience and worship to the Lord. And if you're committed to your rightful responsibilities, in a sense you're serving. And God says, "You're the greatest!"

Not all women will agree with me. Not all my friends do! But if you feel that for now God has called you to be a homemaker, let me encourage you. I invite you to experience the privilege of serving, the art of loving and giving and the development of your creativity. But primarily, I invite you to help keep before the world God's visual aid of what Christ is to the Church, His Body.

Ephesians 5:23 says, "For the husband is the head of the wife, even as Christ is the head of the church . . ." (*KJV*). If families are ripped apart, each going his or her own way, or if within marriage the husband and wife see themselves as two directors, two heads, Satan succeeds in destroying God's picture of what Christ is to us—our Head.

You can blame Eve if you like, but the fact remains! Because sin entered the world, God gave husbands the right to be head over woman, or as Genesis 3:16 states, to be "master" over woman. True, in our spiritual lives we are equal—in that real self, where Christ dwells, in that new man where there is neither Jew nor Greek, slave nor free, male or female (see Galatians 3:28). This is a spiritual law.

But there is also a moral law which deals with our "old man." Until our salvation is completed on that day when Christ calls us to Himself, we must live with our fallen nature, under the curse. Women still bring forth children in pain (or "sorrow"), the snake still crawls on its belly, man still has to work by the sweat of his brow, anyone with a garden is daily reminded by the rocks, weeds, and thistles, that indeed the ground is cursed, and death overtakes us all (see Genesis 3:14-19).

Jesus, Himself, in Mark 10:6 reiterates that "from the very first he [God] made man and woman . . ."

He made woman to be a companion and help for the man because it was not good for him to be alone.

Which brings us to the homemaker! There are still those women who enjoy their place in God's order of things, who see themselves as a "help meet for their husband," as homemakers, not just as housewives or housekeepers. It is to these women this book is lovingly dedicated.

Recently a young mother of four wrote to me for help in her role as a homemaker. As a mother of two girls and two boys and twenty-six years of homemaking experience, I'd like to share with you what we shared through our letters.

I believe Joyce's fresh honesty and insights will delight you. I trust you'll find my housekeeping hints, recipes, and thoughts from the Word helpful. Our prayer is that you will catch a glimpse of the homemaker's high calling and in our letters find your *invitation to greatness.*

2

A New Friend

2

꧁◌◌◌꧂

Dear Mrs. Steven,

Two days ago I bought and read your book *What Kids Katch from Parents*.[1] I enjoyed it very much. I hope you don't mind if I write to you as a friend. For some reason I feel very close to you and I really need some help.

First of all, I realize I don't know how to keep house. My mother tried to teach me by giving me jobs around the house, but all I learned was how to take orders. After my marriage, it didn't take me long to discover I don't know how to make good use of my time. I'm disorganized and I never know where to start.

Secondly, I don't have a vacuum cleaner, and most of the floors in our old eight-room house (six down

1. Copyright © 1976, Harvest House Publishers, Irvine, California 92714.

and two up) are carpeted with indoor-outdoor carpeting. I also don't have a washer, dryer or dishwasher.

The third problem is the children. My oldest is in the first grade. I have to drive her to school every morning when it's too cold to walk the mile. My next child, age five, goes to afternoon kindergarten so I drive her to school at 12:30, then drive back to pick them up at 3:15. Next comes our three-year-old who needs a lot of help and attention, and then there's the baby, seven months old. I nurse him every four hours but am trying to work towards three meals a day. He's a nonsleeper who seldom takes a nap for more than a half hour.

I'm also a big part of the problem. I have a relaxed, good-natured disposition and seldom get angry or nervous, but I'm not very fast-moving and am prone to put things off.

My husband is a lot like me—he puts things off, too! But he's a terrific help. When he gets home from work he pitches in, washes dishes, sweeps, or helps out where he can. He takes the laundry to the laundromat once a week. He almost never complains about the way the house looks, but I don't think he really understands how much I want to improve things. However, I know he feels badly that there isn't much we can do for the house on his salary.

There are lots of other things that make it hard. We live in a small town and I don't have any friends close by. I'm so ashamed of this house, I can't invite anyone over. I don't even invite my parents over!

I hope you don't get the impression that I am a

whining, complaining, lazy housewife. I'm happy and grateful to be a housewife and I love my family very much. I feel that keeping a neat, clean home is so very important. I want to make things pleasant and comfortable for the people I love. I want them to be proud of their home; to be able to invite their friends over.

God seems to be calling me to be so many things—a good mother, a good wife, a nutritionist, an economist, and an efficient housekeeper. I want to do everything well and pray about it a lot. But right now I'm confused, discouraged, and just plain bone-tired. I feel like I never have enough time, enough rest, enough money, enough energy.

I will appreciate any and all the advice you might have. I just can't see any solution to the problem. Thank you for reading my letter. And thank you for your book.

In our Saviour,

Joyce

P.S. I almost forgot. How can I help teach my children to be more responsible? I've totally failed to get them to assume any responsibility. But what can I expect, with my example?

3

❦⊙⦿⊙❦

Walking With
The Lord

3

✦

My dear Joyce,

Your letter brightened my day! I loved your openness. And feeling you could write to me as a friend for help is one of the nicest compliments I've ever received!

I recently read that when a person is *really* seeking help, the battle is half won. So I'm excited! I've already been praying for you and praising God for what He has begun to do in your life.

There's so much I would like to share with you. But rather than exhaust you all at one sitting, I'll break up my comments into several letters and together let's explore what God desires for us as His children.

Our walk with the Lord is similar to a house. If we try to get it in order all at once, after a buildup of clutter, it overwhelms us. It's easier to go step by step and room by room. The old adage, "A woman's work is never done; she works from dawn 'til setting sun," can also be said of our spiritual lives. We can't clean our homes and say, "There, that's it! Now I can relax for the rest of my life." Maybe for the rest of the day, but tomorrow there are dishes, unmade beds, dirty laundry and things to pick up and put away. And when we clean up our spiritual lives, we can never say, "That's it!" There must be a continual daily cleansing.

In his book *The Healing of Persons*, Paul Tournier says, "I can only say that the spiritual world is no different from everything else in this world: No step forward is maintained unless it is followed by further steps. He who does not go forward, goes back. Physical, psychical, and spiritual health is not a haven in which we can take refuge in a sort of final security, but a daily battle."[2]

It's easier to accept the challenge of daily cleansing for both our lives and home if we realize we're in a battle. But where and how do we begin? Good news! God has already promised to instruct, teach, and guide us. Psalm 32:8 says: "I will instruct you [says the Lord] and guide you along the best pathway for your life; I will advise you and watch your progress." Don't just claim this as promised direction for life's *big* decisions. God is interested in every aspect of our lives. One only has to read His

2. Paul Tournier, Condensed edition (Westchester, Illinois, 1967) p. 6.

instructions in Exodus, Leviticus and Numbers regarding the tabernacle, sin, and offerings to see His love of details!

Maybe you're like me. You read a verse, perhaps even memorize it, but it doesn't do too much for you until you study and claim it for yourself.

Recently I looked in our concordance for meanings of the individual words in Psalm 32:8 and suddenly the verse came alive. It's changed my whole way of praying for God's will in my life.

I found when God says He's going to *instruct* me, He's saying, "I'm going to cause you to act wisely." "Guiding me with His eye" means, "He's watching my progress."

Armed with other Hebrew definitions, I rewrote Psalm 32:8 in words that communicated to me: "As I go along living my life, God is not only going to *show* me how to act wisely, He's going to *cause* me to act wisely; and as He watches my progress, He's going to be beside me, coaching me."

This all sounds fantastic, but we both know there are many times when we don't act wisely and God seems anything but near. What's the problem?

I found the answer in the preceding verses. In Psalm 32:1 David says, "What happiness for those whose guilt has been forgiven! What joys when sins are covered over!" In other words, David addresses this psalm to a particular group—the forgiven ones.

To be a recipient of God's promise in Psalm 32:8:

Step number one: We need our sins forgiven. And this can only come about through faith in Jesus Christ. "Brothers! Listen! In this man Jesus, there is forgiveness of your sins! Everyone who trusts in him is freed from all guilt and declared righteous—something the Jewish law could never do" (Acts 13:38, 39).

Step number two: No duplicity. Psalm 32:2, in the *King James Version*, says that a man is blessed "in whose spirit there is no guile." The meaning of guile or duplicity is to speak or act differently at different times in relation to the same thing. It's the exact opposite of the Christians in Acts 2:46 who had "singleness of heart."

When God forgives us and we belong to Him, He wants our actions to show it ("Be ye doers of the word and not hearers only . . .", James 1:22, *KJV*].

Step number three: Confession, as found in Psalm 32:5: ". . . I finally admitted all my sins to you and stopped trying to hide them. I said to myself, 'I will confess them to the Lord.' And you forgave me! All my guilt is gone."

God forgives us when we invite Him into our lives. But there must also be a daily confessing of sin in order to keep our minds and lives uncluttered. That's the battle! Only as we confess our sin is our relationship with Him restored and we can say with David, in Psalm 32:7: "O Lord, you are my hiding place. Everything is okay again. When I'm living close to you, you're going to be right here beside me to keep me out of trouble."

When we're in this position, we can *praise* Him for His promised leading—even when we have to wait for an answer or direction. We can rest in the knowledge He's causing us to act wisely, coaching us when we lack wisdom. When we are rightly related to Him and understand that our lives are under His watchful care, we can accept where He's placed us, hard as it may be. We can praise Him for our husband, children, home, and everything in it (even if it is sparse and less than what many of our friends have) because we know these are His gifts to us. We begin to see that cleaning house, rearing children, being a good wife, whatever we do, has eternal value. Our loving Father, who is living *in* us now, is preparing us for the time we'll go to *live* with Him. We may find ourselves moving away from this close position with our Heavenly Father, and have to learn these lessons all over again—many times—but it's good to know He stands ready to receive us back!

Our goal in life should be as Paul states in 2 Corinthians 10:13 to "measure up to God's plan for us," not what we think is our "right." The way God perfects us to fit into His plan for us is not always easy or pleasant. Sometimes it is through suffering, bereavement, or disease. Other times it may be through poverty, injustice, or extreme cruelty on the part of someone else. "Whatever the circumstance," says Paul Tournier, "God wants to use it as an instrument for the purification and edifying of the Christian character."[3]

When we get our life in perspective and view it as God's gift to us for His purposes, I think we can get on with effective Christian living. The apostle Paul challenges us in Philippians 3:13 when he says, ". . . forgetting the past and looking forward to what lies ahead." Paul Tournier says: "Living with God means living the present hour which he gives us,

3. Ibid, p. 29.

putting our whole heart into what he expects of us in that hour, and leaving the past and the future to him, to whom they belong.''[4] It's good to know our life is not a series of mismatched, unexplainable events. It's a series of preparations—preparations for our future life with Him.

In my next letter I want to give you a few practical housecleaning hints and share what we've learned about living on less. We'll tackle the hub of our homes—the kitchen—and the hub of our lives—our minds. Until then I'm praying for you.

Lovingly in Christ,

Norma

4. Ibid, p. 6.

4

※◎⊙◎∾

Housecleaning
Hints for Kitchen
and Mind

4

⁕

Dear Joyce,

Are you ready? Let's begin to tackle our disordered lives and homes.

There are three things we can do to clean up the clutter in our minds. One is prayer. Through prayer God changes negative, debilitating, unproductive thoughts into positive, active, healthy actions.

Corrie Ten Boom gives a graphic example of this in her book, *The Hiding Place*. When she and her sister were moved to Ravensbruck prison camp during World War II, the barracks were more than she thought she could bear. However, her sister Betsie immediately called on the Lord to show them how to live in such a place. Suddenly she remembered their morning Bible reading in 1 Thessalonians 5. "Rejoice evermore" (verse 16, KJV). "In every thing give thanks . . ." (verse 18, *KJV*). And Betsie was even able to give God thanks for the fleas!

This took more than a casual prayer life. Just before this event Corrie comments: "More and more the distinction between prayer and the rest of life seemed to be vanishing for Betsie."

Like eating and sleeping, prayer should be a natural part of life. But to be this, it must be a daily habit. Begin each day, those first waking moments, by greeting the Lord. And if you can't spend an extended time with the Lord right then, make a time when you can. In this way you'll begin to develop your friendship with the Lord.

Secondly, Bible reading and study. Psalm 119:11 says, "I have thought much about your words, and stored them in my heart so that they would hold me back from sin." If, as James 1:14 tells us, sin begins in our thoughts, we need God's Word stored there to call to mind when temptation strikes.

But Bible reading and study is more than an antidote for sin. It's the other half of our friendship with Christ. We learn more about a friend when *they're* talking than when *we're* talking, and one way God speaks to us is through His Word.

Right now your time is extremely limited. For the present, until your children are older, you will find it difficult to get away to a Bible study group during the week or do extensive Bible study on your own. Churches often have a Sunday morning Bible class and nursery care is usually provided. But don't let this take the place of your own daily Bible reading. To go along with your reading you might enjoy a daily devotional book like "Our Daily Bread," offered free through Radio Bible Class, P.O. Box 22,

Grand Rapids, Michigan 49501.

The prophet Jeremiah said that God's Words "are what sustain me; they are food to my hungry soul. They bring joy to my sorrowing heart and delight me" (15:16). What an antidote for depression!

The third way to get rid of clutter buildup in our minds is meditation. And like everything else in life, this also takes effort. There's a great promise in Psalm 1:3 for those who meditate on God's laws: "They are like trees along a river bank bearing luscious fruit each season without fail. Their leaves shall never wither, and all they do shall prosper."

Isaiah 26:3 says, "He will keep in perfect peace all those who trust in him, whose thoughts turn often to the Lord!" Brother Lawrence, a seventeenth century monk, learned how to keep his mind occupied with Christ and shares how he did this in a little book entitled, *The Practice of the Presence of God.* In letters to a friend who desired to know the method he used to arrive at a "habitual sense of God's presence," he wrote: " . . . at all times, every hour, every minute, even in the height of my business [Brother Lawrence washed dishes in a monastery] I drove away from my mind everything that was capable of interrupting my thought of God." Through this practice of keeping in the "presence of God" he could say, "I possess God in as great tranquility as if I were upon my knees at the blessed sacrament."

In his letter to the church at Philippi, Paul gives the Christians practical help in keeping their minds on Christ when he tells them (see Philippians 4:8) to think on these things:

1. What is true, good and right
2. Pure and lovely things
3. Fine, good qualities in others
4. All you can praise God for
5. All you can be glad about

Proverbs 23:7 KJV tells us that "as a man thinks in his heart, so is he." The mind is where it all begins—positive or negative, loving or hateful, productive or unproductive, acceptance or rejection. It's the hub all right! Which brings us to the kitchen—a great place to keep the mind clean while washing dishes (I don't have a dishwasher either!), cooking, baking, ironing, or scrubbing the floor.

I've called the kitchen the hub of our homes because that's where so much of what goes on in the home takes place. Like a bad habit, a messy kitchen takes time to put in order. And like a bad habit, to get rid of it, we have to start inside out!

Let's tackle the cupboards first. I line my shelves with self-adhesive paper. It's expensive at first but easier to keep clean and lasts longer than paper.

Have a special place for each category. Keep least used items on top shelves or hard to reach places. Store everyday-dishes on lower shelves, next to the sink, where you can put them away easily. Keep glasses together on one side, plates, bowls and cups on the other side. If you're short of cupboard space, Rubber Maid has great dish stackers.

Don't mix food items in with the dishes; especially those items like salt, pepper, spices, butter, jams, syrups, sauces and baking items. Have a special handy shelf for these, as this shelf will need to be washed more frequently than the others. At least once a year, preferably twice, go right through all your kitchen cupboards. Take everything out, shelf by shelf, wash well, get rid of unused items, and (with food) outdated items.

Keep cereals and crackers together in a dry place. Your canned foods should be stored neatly where you can readily see what you have on hand. Keep dishcloths and towels together in a drawer. A drawer is also a great place to store different sized plastic containers and lids. Pots and pans should be kept in cupboards near the stove.

Another trick for keeping the kitchen in order is to have a "junk" drawer. I keep one drawer for all those little things you never know what to do with. Rather than have them clutter all over the place, I have a flat plastic divided container which fits inside the drawer for those rubber bands, paper clips, buttons, box tops, coupons, nails, screws—you name it—and this drawer I clean out, putting things in their proper place, several times a year.

Household cleaning items should be kept together out of reach of your youngsters. Use a cardboard box in your broom closet for dusters or old rags used for cleaning.

Don't let your refrigerator or oven go too long before cleaning them. How often you do this is up to you, but take time to do it.

Use up those leftovers in your refrigerator and throw out spoiled items. It's all part of getting rid of that buildup. And be sure to get your husband or someone to help you move the refrigerator every few months. It's amazing how much dust collects behind them in just a few weeks.

I use a "spray on" oven cleaner for my oven but you might prefer one of the other products on the market. Be sure to put paper on the floor and use rubber gloves. It's a messy job but it feels so good when it's done!

Sweep your kitchen floor every day. Right after doing the breakfast dishes is a great time. Wash it at least once a week. I use a pine-scented disinfectant in the water to wash my kitchen and bathroom floors. Not only does it disinfect, it smells so clean!

When you finish with the dishes (which I like to do right after meals), check the cupboards for handprints or other messes. Be sure to check the stove top. Wash the trays under the burners if there are spills so they won't be twice as hard to remove later. I use bleach to clean my sinks every two to three weeks as they're old and other cleansers don't do a complete job. Bleach is also great for cleaning ceramic tile counter tops.

Keep kitchen counters as free as possible of clutter. Take time to make a place for things to fit into your cupboards. In short, the more you take care of today, the less you'll have to tackle tomorrow!

I promised to share something about stretching the budget. One good way is to shop wisely, and don't hesitate to ask the Lord for wisdom whenever you go to the market. Prices vary in supermarkets and it does pay to shop in one that has the best overall prices. Don't go shopping when you're hungry—you're bound to buy more! Buy only the essentials for well-balanced meals. Save the frills for special occasions. Buy fresh rather than frozen foods when possible; prepared foods are convenient, but it really doesn't take too much longer to start from scratch—and it tastes better!

Look for the least expensive whole chickens, which, when doctored up, are just as tasty as the more expensive packets of cut up chicken pieces. To serve: wash; cut into serving pieces; coat with flour, salt (garlic or regular), pepper (The easiest way I've found to do this is to put the flour, salt and pepper into a paper bag and drop in the chicken, a piece at a time. Hold the bag tightly shut, and shake well.); brown in a small amount of fat in the pressure cooker. After the chicken pieces are well-browned, pour in one cup water, put on the lid and pressure cook for 15 minutes after the pressure is up. The chicken is not only well done, but tasty, with a delicious gravy to serve over rice or potatoes.

Having trouble cooking rice that isn't a globby mess? My father-in-law, a professional chef, taught me this fail-proof method: Use a three-quart pot; fill two-thirds with water; add rice (one-and-a-half cups should do for your family); bring to boil. Boil rapidly until done, about 15 minutes. If you keep a metal spoon in the pot while boiling the rice, it's less likely to boil over. Drain the rice in a collander or strainer. Rinse well with cold water; then hot. Drain well and put back in the pot. Add two tablespoons margarine or butter, salt and pepper to taste. Heat through on low heat, stirring to keep from sticking.

A great way to use hamburger is to season with a

package of Kikkoman Instant Teriyaki Sauce Mix. Follow directions on the package and either grill or broil your hamburger patties.

My family loves the way my mother fixes hamburger. She adds about half a cup of chopped onion to a pound of hamburger, pepper, salt ("a generous amount," she always says!) and about a quarter of a cup of milk. Mix well and fry in well-heated fry pan until browned on both sides.

Try using hamburger patties with Kraft's macaroni and Cheese Dinner plus a green vegetable. It's quick, nutritious and inexpensive, and a change from the all-American hamburger in a bun!

For variety, make hamburger meatballs and gravy. Season the hamburger with salt, pepper, one-half chopped onion, 1 clove garlic (minced) or 1/8 teaspoon instant minced garlic, 2 tablespoons milk. To stretch, add 1/3 cup bread crumbs or rolled oats. Mix well and form into balls the size of a walnut. Coat with flour. Fry in a small amount of hot fat until browned. Remove meatballs. Drain off fat. Put the pan back on the burner, add 1/2 cup water and scrape all the browned drippings from the bottom of the pan. Add one can mushroom soup. Mix well. Put meatballs back in the pan and cook for 20 to 30 minutes, stirring occasionally. Add more water if the gravy is too thick. Serve with mashed or boiled potatoes, a vegetable, and a tossed or jell-o salad.

An inexpensive cut is a beef chuck, 7-bone beef roast. It's under a dollar a pound, and is tasty. Brown the roast in small amount of fat in an electric skillet or fry pan with a lid. Dissolve one package of Lipton's or Wyler's onion soup mix in one-third cup water. Pour over browned meat. Put on the lid and simmer on low heat for one hour. Turn about every twenty minutes, checking to see if the water has evaporated. If so, add a little more. When I turn it over the first time, I scrape up the onion pieces and put them on top of the roast again. If you cook potatoes to serve with this, save the potato water. When the meat is done, remove, and add potato water to drippings in pan. To thicken, mix one tablespoon cornstarch with two tablespoons water in cup. Stir until dissolved and well mixed. Pour slowly into boiling gravy, stirring constantly until desired thickness.

I like to make use of my oven for more than one item, so if I bake a chicken in the oven, I also bake potatoes and tomatoes. Use the better chicken fryers as there's less waste. Place the chicken in a Pyrex baking dish or metal pan; season with salt, pepper and garlic; dot with butter or margarine and bake at 350 degrees for one hour, turning once after one-half hour.

Or you might like to use Shake 'n Bake which is also quick and easy. Bake potatoes at the same time, but choose medium to small potatoes or they may not get cooked through in an hour. Scrub the potatoes well, rub with butter or margarine, prick with fork (so they won't pop!) or wrap in foil and bake.

When tomatoes are in season, wash, cut in half, season with salt, pepper, a sprinkle of sugar, dab of margarine or butter, and sprinkle with Parmesan cheese. Place in shallow pan (a metal pie plate is great) and bake the last half hour the chicken and potatoes are cooking. Serve with a green vegetable and salad and you have a colorful, delicious meal!

If you want desserts, keep them simple: jell-o, puddings, ice cream, sherbets, fruit (fresh when it's in season). Children are often satisfied with a cookie and my favorite recipe is one simply called "Good Cookies" and it makes approximately 100!

Good Cookies

2 cups brown sugar	3 ½ cups flour
1 cup margarine	1 teaspoon soda
1 cup oil	1 teaspoon cream of tartar
1 egg	1 cup Rice Krispies
1 teaspoon vanilla	1 cup coconut
1 teaspoon salt	1 cup oats

1 cups nuts

Method: Blend sugar, margarine, oil, egg, and vanilla. Sift in flour, soda, salt, cream of tartar. Add remaining ingredients. Drop by teaspoon or roll in balls and press down with fork (do not make too large). Bake at 350 degrees for 12 to 15 minutes, or until golden brown. Do not grease cookie sheet.

Remember, shopping wisely is shopping frugally. Stay with store name brands on canned foods. We buy day-old bread at a bakery outlet. Supermarkets also have day-old bakery items. Mix your milk with half powdered milk. Buy large economy sizes. Experiment with different brands. Palmolive or Ivory Liquid for dishwashing, while more expensive, are cheaper in the long run because they go further than less expensive dishwashing liquids. To make bar soap last longer, store with the wrappers removed. The air dries the soap and makes it harder. The harder the soap the longer it lasts. Save paper and plastic bags. (Get a special place for them to avoid clutter!) Plastic containers from margarine, honey, or cottage cheese are great for leftovers as are some of the wide-mouthed bottles.

Overwhelmed? Remember Psalm 32:8. He's going to cause you to act wisely! Each day ask Him for wisdom for all you have to do. Another favorite promise of mine is Psalm 37:23: "The steps of good men are directed by the Lord." And read on to verse 24: "If they fall it isn't fatal, for the Lord holds them with his hand."

He's right there, with "His eye upon you," to help you on to effective living for Him! Until next week,

Your sister in Christ,

Norma

5

❦

Getting Back
Your "Oomph"

5

❧❦❧

Dear Joyce,

How are things this week? Is the kitchen becoming easier to put in order now that the cupboards are? I didn't mention that I find doing dishes right after meals and wiping the stove and counter tops at the same time makes me feel the house is cleaner all over! It's something like the feeling I get when I have a time with the Lord first thing in the morning. Somehow the day is started in the right direction! Now, let's move to our room for the week—the living room.

If you're like us, without a family or rumpus room, your living room is well used. It's a place for relaxation, and that brings up disciplined living. It's easy to let precious hours and minutes slip by and then wonder where the day went! If the hours spent in TV watching or reading newspapers or magazines outweighs time needed for personal and family devotions, good reading material, household duties and time spent with your children, husband, and friends, I think you will agree that we need to reevaluate our priorities.

Because God is our rightful owner we need to realize that our time is not our own. Jesus said, "Deny yourself. Take up your cross and follow me" (see Matthew 16:24). This is why I always ask the Lord to help me use my time wisely—it's His! And it's a precious commodity!

There's another part of disciplined living—keeping physically fit. While daily spiritual exercise is of prime importance, daily physical exercise is also beneficial. 1 Timothy 4:8 says: "Bodily exercise is all right, but spiritual exercise is much more important and is a tonic for all you do." This doesn't mean that we shouldn't bother with physical fitness. Rather Paul is telling Timothy to get his priorities straight.

From experience I know how washed out you must feel from your closely spaced pregnancies. In order to get some "oomph" back into that tired body, exercise is a must. If the weather is not too extreme, take a daily brisk walk. If you can't get out, run in place, touch your toes, do waist-bending exercises. Start with a few, then slowly increase each day. Getting into a regular routine is difficult, but once you get over the first few days and persevere, you'll feel so much better and find you don't tire as quickly. I also find lying down for ten or fifteen minutes during the day helps. Try it even if you have to let the baby fuss.

One thing that makes me want to watch what I take

into my mind and body, and to have it in good working order is the realization that Christ is in me! Read 1 Corinthians 3:16, 17. It's awesome to think we are the temple of God!

Now, for some practical help with cleaning the living room. The nicest thing you can do for your home is *love*. Our living room has faded drapes, secondhand furniture, and dark, low nap carpeting like the indoor-outdoor type you mentioned you have. I have tried to brighten it with plants and, more recently, we've been able to add some wall shelves which help tremendously. Yet even before we had these extras, people would come in and say, "This is such a nice place," or "It's so peaceful." And these remarks came from people with beautiful homes and furnishings! I could never understand it until one day a lady, after commenting on our home, said, "But it's more than what you have or how it's fixed [I guess she began to notice we didn't have all that much!], it's . . . it's . . . why, I think it's love I feel!"

The next thing you can do to help a living room's appearance is to keep it neat. If the children play with their toys in the living room, keep a cardboard box handy. My husband never liked to see a messy living room so I'd let the children play; then, just before he was due home, I'd throw the toys in the box. One side comment: as the children grow older they can be taught not to drag everything out at once!

Newspapers have a way of making a room look messy, so have a special place to put or pile them. It's not easy to keep things straight with four little ones, but keeping the clutter to a minimum helps you, your husband, and friends to enjoy your home more. If you have to let everything else go, at least keep your living room in order.

Once a week I go completely through the house with what I call a "thorough" cleaning. Dust the furniture with a soft cloth. I use Johnson's Clean and Shine, which does just what its name implies, or a heavier furniture polish or lemon oil to cover scratched furniture.

By now I'm trusting you have a vacuum. If not, sweep the floor before dusting. Be sure to dust windowsills and ledges. Look for cobwebs in corners. It's not necessary to move the sofa or other heavy items each week, but do move them periodicially. Vacuum under the sofa cushions each week or dust underneath to remove dirt. If your sofa cushions are reversable, rearrange them each week to avoid wear in a certain spot.

To brighten your sofa or rug, shampoo them with one of the commercial cleaners, following directions. You can rent a rug shampooer at a supermarket and you should do this once a year if possible.

In the morning, before making breakfast, tidy up the living room by picking up shoes, clothes, dishes, books, papers, pencils, or other stray items, and put them where they belong, or in a pile to put away later on in the morning. In this way the living room never looks too disastrous.

Don't let your sofa pile up with laundry, jackets, or toys. I insist the children take their things to their rooms. It's an endless battle, but they do finally get into the habit! Get into the habit of putting the laundry where it belongs as soon as possible. Keep mending in one place, ironing in another. If you remember in my book, *What Kids Katch from Parents*, I mention having special places for things in order to be more organized.

Make a place by the back door to hang coats, jackets or sweaters. In your kind of weather you need a place to store boots and extra pairs of shoes. It takes time, but insisting the children put their things where they belong finally pays off. That is, if you're being careful to do the same!

Make your living room cozy by adding a few plants, books, knicknacks or pictures in attractive ways. They don't have to be expensive. Paste a pretty scene or flower picture on colored construction paper, leaving a border. Group several small pictures together. With a little creativity you can do wonders! Cover old pillows with bright gingham or calico. use an old trunk for a coffee table, end table, or to sit in a corner with books or plants on top. When I'm stuck for an idea, I ask the Lord to help me. After all, He's the author of creativity! I think effective Christian living is not only disciplined living, but also creative living.

When I couldn't afford wallpaper for the kitchen, I cut out flowers from self-adhesive paper and stuck them on the wall in a border pattern. When I wanted something for my bathroom wall, I framed two greeting cards with beautiful scenes. On another wall I grouped six different-sized wooden plaques on which I glued some shells I had sitting in a closet. The plaques, advertised to be used for decoupage, were on sale for five for $1.00! I sanded them, rubbed in some stain and sprayed a bit of gold on the edges. If you don't have time for decoupage, you could glue greeting card figures or a few dried flowers on the boards and spray with clear lacquer. Make a grouping by using a colorful poster along with items from a rummage sale or secondhand shop—an old picture, plate, key, whatever. Use your imagination!

When your living room is in order, you'll feel more like entertaining. Why not ask one or two couples over for an evening? It's not necessary to have anything fancy. Make a batch of those Good Cookies mentioned in my last letter, a pot of coffee or tea, and you're on your way! Or why not try this easy lemon cake. Everyone always loves it.

Lemon Cake
1 pkg. white or yellow cake mix
1 3 oz. box lemon jell-o
3/4 cup water
1/2 cup salad oil
4 eggs unbeaten

Method: Place all ingredients in bowl. Beat with a mixer for 3 minutes. Pour into a greased & floured 9 x 13 pan. Bake at 350 degrees, 25-30 minutes. Remove from oven. Prick holes in cake with fork and spread with the following glaze.

Lemon Glaze
1/3 cup lemon juice
2 cups powdered sugar
2 tbsp. margarine, melted
1 tbsp. water

Blend lemon juice into the powdered sugar. Add the margarine and water. Mix well.

If you're ever in need of a spur-of-the-moment snack, serve crackers and cheese; toasted English muffins topped with margarine (or butter) and jam or jelly; or toast bread and top with brown sugar and cinnamon.

Besides having fellowship with other couples, you and your husband need to have time away from the family. If you don't have a baby-sitter, pray and trust God to help you find one. Even if you get away by yourselves for a cup of coffee or a sundae at a local coffee shop once a week, you'll be better able to cope with pressures.

I'm praying for God to provide you with a washer and dryer. In this way you can wash more often and your husband will be free to do some of those never-ending fix-it items. Remember, God wants to and promises to supply all your needs—and we've also experienced that He delights to sometimes give us a *want* or two! I have a lot of entertaining to do, but have never had a decent set of dishes. Our first years in Mexico were extremely hard financially, yet God met needs, great and small. When I needed some new clothes, fellow missionaries took me shopping at a secondhand dress shop and I found two lovely dresses. In 1969 we were given a brand new station wagon. It now has 121,000 miles on it, and I admit that sometimes we get frustrated with the repairs, but we are excited about what God is going to do to provide us with another car. Just recently we were given a piano. I could share many other exciting times the Lord has supplied super abundantly above anything we could ask or think. So keep praying and trusting! I don't believe we should look to God as a benevolent grandfather who will give us our every fancy or whim. But He knows our hearts and He loves to give good gifts to those who walk uprightly (Psalm 84:11).

Happy cleaning! And happy hospitality! Romans 12:13 tells us to "get into the habit of inviting guests home for dinner," while 1 Peter 4:9 says to "cheerfully share your home with those who need a meal or a place to stay for the night."

I'm looking forward to hearing from you again. Until next week,

Your sister in Christ,

Norma

6

Practical
Things First?

6

❧❦❧

Dear Norma,

Thank you so much for your letter. I can't tell you how much it meant to me. Your words came at just the right time, too. I really needed your encouragement the past ten days.

Our church's director of youth and music and his wife were chaperones at a youth retreat last weekend and we took care of their three small children. It was a job taking care of seven children, but you would have been proud of me! I managed everything with a minimum of fuss. I couldn't have done it alone so I know God was with me.

This week has been hard also. My oldest child has been sick with a virus all week. In fact the whole school was finally closed because of the epidemic.

And we are right in the middle of a crisis with our baby. He has always been a light sleeper and for the past couple of months I have been taking him to bed with me so I could rest. Now we are trying to break the habit. The doctor said to put him to bed and let him cry. Last night he cried all night! It upsets me so much, but I'm convinced it is for his good in the long run. Could you please pray for him?

Speaking of prayers, thank you so much for yours on my behalf. To know another Christian is concerned enough to take my problems and needs to our Father has been most encouraging. And it is helping!

No major changes yet, but a few small steps in the right direction. I now have a table in the kitchen. It means a lot less running back and forth at mealtime. Also the baby's high chair is on linoleum instead of the carpet! We are also trying to establish regular jobs for which the children can be responsible.

I wanted to ask you for your advice on a budget problem. My husband wants to buy a motorcycle and race it in motocross races this summer. I understand that if he does, it means not being able to do some of the things I want to. But I also know how important it is to him. It is a very old dream—almost an obsession. He is a hard worker and does the best he can for the children and I want him to get the motorcycle. My mother feels he is being selfish. Do you think the practical things should *always* come first?

I am excited about my "correspondence course" in homemaking—as I like to think of it! I believe God is speaking to me through you. *Your* concern for me has made me feel *His* love and care all the more! I will be working extra hard to not let either one of you down!

Yours in our God who makes weak people strong,

Joyce

7

Responsible Living

7

❦

Dear Joyce,

It was good to hear from you. I know how much time letter writing takes. I was blessed by your kind remarks. Many times we think we have to have a spectacular talent before God can use us. But I've found that He just wants us to give out what He's given us. It's a special joy to know that something of what I'm sharing in these letters will be a help to you. I've been praying daily for you and your family and will especially remember the baby. I'm glad you're putting into practice your doctor's wise advice.

One of our children was a light sleeper and we started out rocking her to put her to sleep. The result was that we would sometimes end up rocking her over an hour to keep her from crying. We finally had to end up doing what you're doing with your baby. It's nerve-wracking, but hang in there! Children learn at a young age who's boss!

I'm glad to see you want your children to be responsible for certain chores. Remember, don't give them too much to do too soon or they'll become discouraged. Be sure they not only understand *what* you want but *how* to go about doing it. It may take a few weeks or even months, but as you work *with* them, they'll soon learn how to do it on their own.

Responsible living is another facet of effective Christian living. Responsibility means to be accountable, answerable, able to respond to any claim. Because God is our rightful owner, he has the claim to us and it is to Him that we are accountable.

In Romans 14:12 we read, "Yes, each of us will give an account of himself to God." How will we answer? Can we say that He asked too much of us when Paul tells us in Philippians 4:13 that we can do *all* things through Christ's strength? Or when we give an account to God, when we see Him face to face, can we give the excuse, "Well, I gave it a try, but it was too much effort," when Colossians 3:23 tells us to do everything cheerfully (enthusiastically, eagerly, warmly, seriously) just as though you were working for the Lord? Responsibility to the Lord is not an option for the Christian!

Once when my husband was away for five weeks in South America, I began to wonder how I was ever going to cope with all the responsibilities facing me. As I drove to my part-time job at a bookstore one day, I thought, "What's the matter with me? He's the God of the impossible! All things are possible with Him!" And then the Lord put a little chorus in my mind that I sing with great gusto every time I get in a similar situation:

> I can do all things through Christ who
>   strengthens me,
> Who strengthens me with His might.
> He's the God of the impossible
> Of whom nothing is too hard,
> I can do all things through Christ who
>   strengthens me,
> Who strengthens me with His might.

Responsibility also brings up the question of budget. Besides God's claim on our lives, there's a claim on us by the bills that come in each month. If we're responsible, we'll keep up our payments. There are claims on us by our children—a hungry mouth to feed, a kiss on a "hurt," a diaper to change, a discipline to administer. Between husband and wife there are also claims or responsibilities to fill.

As a wife I'm responsible to submit (Ephesians 5:22) and show respect (Ephesians 5:33) to my husband. According to Ephesians 5:25-33, a husband is responsible for married love which is to be as "Christ loved the church and gave Himself for it."

Dwight Hervey Small, in his book, *Design for Christian Marriage*, says, "The whole mystery of creative and reciprocal love is embodied in this principle . . . It is love creating its own response. In loving his wife, the husband causes her to love him in return." Mr. Small suggests five characteristics of what this love should be:

1. Realistic
2. Sacrificial
3. Purposeful
4. Willfull
5. Absolute

I want to touch on the second point. We know how costly Christ's love was for us. And God says this is how a husband is to love his wife. To quote Mr. Small: "It means that nothing shall have priority over their responsibility to fulfill the needs of their wives."

Which brings us to the motorcycle. It is not your husband's desire for the motorcycle that's wrong, but perhaps the timing is wrong. I don't think practical things need always come first but perhaps in your situation right now, if some impractical spending is to be done, it should benefit more than one individual. Our family lives with an unspoken motto, "First things first," yet at times, to save me making a meal we'll eat out or buy Kentucky Fried Chicken. We've gone away for a weekend, taken good vacations, and sent the children to camp when there have been other pressing practical needs.

I hope you both pray, looking to the Lord for His direction, before you make a decision. And while I mentioned a wife submitting to a husband, don't forget that in Ephesians 5:21 we're told to submit to one another. In this way a husband won't lord it over his wife, but will take her into account in all decisions made. If an agreement can't be reached, and a decision is needed, only then should the husband have the final word. Otherwise a good rule to practice is to "agree to disagree." But actually the husband has the greater responsibility. He is to love sacrificially, looking out for his wife's needs before his own!

If after discussing all the pros and cons you decide to go ahead, no one need make you feel guilty. Parents often neglect to see the importance of children making their own decisions, even if it means failure. But remember, no one can make you feel guilty unless you choose to feel guilty. However, guilty feelings can be God trying to tell us something!

With responsible living in mind, let's move on to the dining room.

Mealtimes can be as hectic or as pleasant as we mothers make them. I know many families rarely eat a meal together. If they do, it's in front of the TV. Right now mealtimes for you will be difficult with the baby. I could always count on the baby being fussy just as I sat down to eat. As a result, to this day I eat too quickly—a hangover from the days I had to gulp down my food in order to get up and feed the baby or attend to his or her need!

But even if you aren't able to sit through a whole meal, take that extra time to make mealtimes as pleasant as possible for your family. Set a pretty table. For years all I had was plastic dishes (secondhand at that!) but I made sure the table had a plastic or cloth tablecloth or placemats. We now have a tiny oval table and there's never enough room, but I still insist on a blossom, candle or artificial flower for a centerpiece.

Don't plunk the milk down in the bottle or carton. Put it in a pitcher and put jams and jellies in little bowls or those special jam jars. The more pleasant your table, the better the food seems to taste! I'm glad you were able to get a kitchen table, but don't let that stop you from setting it attractively.

Try to serve your meals around the same time each day. It makes it easier to plan the rest of your day. Also I believe most husbands enjoy a regular supper hour. My husband always says, "I don't mind if supper isn't on time, but at least have the table set. That way I feel supper is at least on its way!"

Meals don't have to be elaborate to be nutritious. Be sure to serve hot cereals for some breakfasts. Vary your breakfasts and vary the cereals. But use the most nutritious cold cereals. Try making your own granola.

Granola

6 cups rolled oats (uncooked)
1 cup coconut
1 cup chopped unblanched almonds (or filberts)
1 cup hulled sunflower seeds (or pumpkin seeds)
1 cup wheat germ
1/2 cup sesame seeds
3/4 cup honey
3/4 cup vegetable oil. Melt these last two ingredients together.

Method: Mix all ingredients and spread in thin layer on cookie sheet. Bake at 325 degrees for 20 minutes. Stir often until crisp and light brown. Add 2 cups raisins or currants. Mix and store in plastic containers.

One thing I haven't scrimped on is fruit juice and fresh fruit. In off seasons I stay with apples and bananas, but supplement these with a greater variety when fruit is in season.

Keep lunches simple. Soup or sandwiches are sufficient. A boiled egg (if you haven't served them for breakfast) and cottage cheese; or a sliced apple and hunks of cheese are great if you're counting calories.

I've already shared some recipes with you, but here's a dandy meal to serve your family or guests.

Lasagna

1 lb. ground beef	1 8 oz. can tomato sauce
2 cloves minced garlic	1 pkg spaghetti sauce mix
1 teaspoon seasoned salt	1/2 lb. lasagna noodles
1/2 teaspoon pepper	1/2 lb. mozzarella cheese
1 1 lb. 12 oz. can tomatoes	1 pint cottage cheese
1/2 cup Parmesan cheese	

Method: Brown meat, drain off grease. Add salt, garlic, pepper. Simmer 10 minutes. Add tomatoes, tomato sauce, spaghetti sauce mix. Stir, cover and simmer 30 minutes. Boil noodles, drain and rinse with cold water. Pour 1/3 meat sauce in 9 x 13 baking dish (or lasagna pan). Cover meat with strips of noodles. Arrange slices of mozzarella cheese and spoonfuls of cottage cheese over noodles. Repeat layer ending with meat sauce and top with Parmesan cheese. Bake in 350 degree oven for 30 minutes.

To serve, cut in serving-size pieces and serve with tossed salad and French bread which has been sliced, spread with garlic butter, wrapped in aluminum foil and heated the last 15-20 minutes the lasagna was cooking. Spruce up a tossed green salad by adding bean sprouts, different lettuces, bits of fresh cauliflower, fresh sliced mushrooms, hulled sunflower seeds, chopped cooked bacon, chopped hard boiled eggs, or sliced cucumbers. Set out two or three salad dressings. Serve lemon cake or spumoni ice cream for dessert and you've a meal fit for a king!

If you want a quick simple salad, drain a can of fruit salad and throw in a handful of miniature marshmallow, If you have time, a favorite jell-o salad in our home is:

Mandarin Orange-Apricot Salad

1 3 oz. box orange jell-o   1 11 oz. can Mandarin
1 cup boiling water   orange segments, drained
           1 cup apricot nectar

Method: Dissolve jell-o in boiling water. Add apricot nectar. When slightly jelled, add the mandarin orange segments, stir, and put into mold.

As for cleaning the dining room, it's much the same as the other rooms. I find that to keep clutter at a minimum I must constantly *pick up and put away*—PUAPA for short! That's where those special places for things help! The weekly "thorough" cleaning makes the job of daily housekeeping easier.

Now that the kitchen, living and dining areas are tidy, we're almost there! It may be that you can't get to the bedrooms each week, but getting into the "PUAPA" habit will make them seem less disastrous. Once I've talked about the bedrooms and bathrooms, I'll tell you how I go about daily and weekly cleaning from start to finish. In the meantime, keep working at the kitchen, living room and dining room, and let me know how you're coming along.

Much love in Christ,

Norma

8

◈

I'm Shaping Up

8

Dear Norma,

I have a lot to tell you. First of all, my kitchen is beginning to shape up! I have nearly all my cabinets cleaned out and reorganized. It's really a good feeling to open those doors and see everything so neat and orderly!

My dining room is also in good shape except for a couple of small things that don't show. Just having those two rooms finally "under control" makes me feel like I really do have a chance to make it as a housewife! I know that the Lord deserves the credit, and I am very thankful to Him for directing me to you. You have been more help to me than you can imagine.

The weather has been warm and spring-like the past week—a real blessing to me. My two older children walk home from school which means I don't have to wake up the boys every afternoon. I am looking forward to having the house in good enough shape that a little straightening in the morning will leave me free to spend the day out in the sun taking the children to the park or working in the garden. There are so many things I would like to do.

Tomorrow I am hoping to go to see my doctor. I suspect that I may be pregnant again!

As I mentioned in my first letter, we don't have any friends close by. We live on a dead-end street and our few neighbors are either elderly or working couples. For a while I attended a Bible study here but failed to make any close, lasting friendships. I just wish sometimes there was somebody around I could call up and say, "Would you watch my children for a while?" It's difficult not to have any place to leave them. Sometimes it's scary. Like when I was pregnant. Once our boy drank some furniture polish. I didn't have a car so I had to call the wife of my husband's boss!

I hope that my letters haven't given you the impression that I'm an unhappy, dissatisfied, or gloomy person! I trust God and am not a worrier and I don't covet other people's lives or possessions. But for as long as I have been a Christian, I'm afraid I'm still not very mature. It bothers me when I see that I'm not using my time and talent to the best of my ability. It's time for me to grow up! I want the Lord to be pleased with me. Thank you so much for all your help. I would never have progressed this far without you (and I still have such a long way to go!).

You were right about not being able to study the

Bible as much as I would like, but I've found a tape ministry that's a great help. I can put on a cassette and listen while I clean house or take a bath or whatever. All the tapes are free and do not have to be returned. Right now I'm on the Philippians study and really enjoy it.

I had a lot of questions to ask you but I'll wait and write again when I get a chance. I hope to finish the kitchen this week and start the living room. I'm a little behind because we all had a virus for a couple of weeks. But I'm determined to catch up!

Love,

Joyce

9

Trustful Living

9

❦

Dear Joyce,

I'm sure by now you're wondering if you're ever going to hear from me again. Sorry I missed last week, but I've been under the weather. Actually, last Monday I was rushed to Emergency as the doctor thought I was having a heart attack. Turned out I wasn't, but I still don't know the cause for the head and chest pain and the pain in my left arm and leg. I can't get an appointment with an internist until next week. I covet your prayers.

I enjoyed hearing from you again. Wondering what the doctor's report revealed! I hope everything is okay. I'm glad you've had the nice weather to help you and that you're finding some of the things I've shared helpful.

In our letters about effective Christian living, I've used the words, frugal, creative, disciplined, responsible, and now I want to add one more—trustful. Effective Christian living means living life "full of trust."

But what exactly does trust mean? To restate the dictionary meaning, it is to "rest my mind of the integrity (or perfection) of another." A successful marriage must have trust between husband and wife. The problem comes when we place *all* our trust in our spouses. If we place all our trust in our mate's integrity (imperfect at best!), what happens when it is momentarily disrupted? Our world begins to fall apart! So then, where is all this trustful living to take place?

Over and over throughout Scripture we're told to "Trust in the Lord." Psalm 118:8 says, "It is better to trust in the Lord than to put confidence in men." I mention this to lead up to an important truth found in Matthew 22:37 and first spoken by God through Moses to the children of Israel. "Love the Lord your God with all your heart, soul, and mind."

For years I grappled to understand how I could love God all that much and still love my husband as I should. It almost seemed to me that to love God first was to be unfaithful to my husband! I know I'll never fully love God as I should until I see Him face to face, but I'm glad for this truth and the truth of Matthew 6:33 which talks about seeking or putting God first. It's so liberating!

God in His wisdom knew how our inconsistencies would provoke, disrupt harmony and, in some cases, destroy others. So He said, "Love me more than anyone else. Place your full trust in me. I'm dependable. I'll never fail you. No matter who or

what disappoints you, I'm sufficient to help you. I'll
lift you up and get you on your feet again. I'll make
the rough road smooth and give peace in place of
turmoil. Give me your worries, hurts and cares. I'll
give you rest.''

Many times I am overwhelmed by God's love for
me. One night when I couldn't sleep, I wrote this
psalm of love.

> I love you Lord,
>   So much.
> From deep inside I yearn to tell you adequately,
> To tell you what you mean
>   To me.
> My finite mind can't grasp the words,
> To somehow let the words pour forth.
> I want to tell you how Your
>   Sweetness,
>   Purity,
>   Peace,
>   Forgiveness,
>   Wholeness,
>   Fulfillment,
> Wrap me in Your Presence.
> You come to me,
> I feel your love
>   While riding in a car,
>   Walking along a street,
>   In the middle of the night,
>   In the yard,
>   Upon my knees;
> I want to hug you!
> One touch, a flash of light I crave,

But I must wait, content to know,
One day your face I'll see.
I'll touch you then, dear Lord;
I'll kiss your feet,
And I hope you'll let me
      Hug you!
I love you, Lord, so much it hurts.
But it's a good hurt, Lord,
And I'll try to wait.

As my love and trust in God grows, so my love for my husband, children, friends—everyone—grows! The more I learn to love and trust Him, the more I give Him my problems to solve. I begin to understand I don't have to carry the burden of trying to make people "better." I can trust God to do that. My job is to love, and that's big enough!

This is my challenge to you for this week. Fill your life, marriage, and home with trustful living!

Now, on to the bedrooms! Your bedroom should be kept as free of clutter as possible. After twenty-six years of marriage, I still believe in keeping as much romance in a marriage as possible! And it's not too romantic to be alone with your husband in a sea of diapers, piles of magazines and other clutter.

Think of your bedroom as your and your husband's private domain. If your door doesn't have a lock, get one! Make the children understand as they get older that they should knock before entering. And you do the same for them (as they get older). Each family member should learn to respect each other's privacy.

One way to keep your bedroom neat is to make your bed first thing in the morning. If your husband is one of those who drop their clothes where they step out of them, hang them up. Don't nag, but sometime when you're discussing things, you could tell him in a nice way that it would help *you* if he hung them up. Don't *attack* his person by telling him he's sloppy. This goes for the children, too!

Once a week I vacuum and dust. If you can't change the sheets and pillowcases every week, once every two weeks is fine. Move the furniture periodically. Get your husband to help with the heavier pieces. If you're doing a daily PUAPA, your bedroom will be one of the easier rooms to clean and keep clean.

Don't forget to turn over your mattress and change it around (top to bottom) a couple of times a year. This saves on wear. Wash blankets or send them to the cleaners at least once a year. I keep pillow covers on my pillows as well as a mattress cover for the mattress. An old pillowcase under the regular case keeps the pillows clean longer. Wash these covers every month or two.

To keep children's bedrooms neat and clean, try hanging a clothes' bar at a level they can reach. This way they can get into the habit of hanging up their clothes. Paint an old trunk or use a sturdy cardboard box for their toys. Have enough shelves, use bricks and varnished or painted boards. If you show children where things belong and let them help you clean their room, they'll soon learn how to clean it by themselves. But don't expect too much before age eight or nine.

After the children learn to keep their rooms fairly

neat on their own, continue to check cupboards, drawers and closets. They let too much accumulate! But don't throw away all their special keepsakes—be sensitive!

Go through the family's clothes periodically to remove or hand down items they've outgrown. Clothes have a way of getting stuck in the bottom of drawers, forgotten, and soon they've outgrown them if you aren't checking every now and then. My children all like their closets and drawers neat because this is how I kept them as they were growing up. It's one of those things they "catch!"

If there are clothes you are saving for later use, don't keep them in with the others. Either store them in boxes or in a garment bag. Children should learn which clothes go well with what so they won't choose purple socks, a red shirt and green blouse to wear together! Remember, you're working toward making them independent adults with an ability to choose wisely in every area of life.

Beware of giving them their independence too soon, however! They'll try while they're young, but hold the line with what you allow them to choose.

In passing, let me recommend a chapter from Paul Tournier's book, *To Resist or To Surrender,* entitled "To Each His Weapon." I believe you'll find his remarks extremely helpful in the whole matter of when and how much freedom one should give to their children.

For instance, if I let our ten-year-old choose what to wear to church, she'd choose jeans! I still insist on a dress Sunday morning as it's the only time she wears one! Perhaps not a strong reason, but it's what I've decided and she needs to understand that while others can wear jeans, that's not my responsibility. Each family is unique, each does things differently, and what we do in our family is what we feel is best. I tell the children we may make mistakes and we're always ready to discuss, but in the end, as mother and father, we are responsible to make them obey us—not us them! I am firmly convinced that small children need a firm, loving hand. Parents who laugh at their small child's antics, do them a disservice. If a child never learns to respect parental authority as a child, it will be difficult, if not impossible, to correct him or her as an adolescent. Be assured, whatever positive effort you put into your home, marriage, and children will be worth it!

I'm praying you'll find another couple with whom you can "exchange" baby-sit. I think it's neat that you desire to "grow up in Him." In Colossians 2:7, we read, "Let your roots grow down into him and draw up nourishment from him. See that you go on growing in the Lord, and become strong and vigorous in the truth you were taught. Let your lives overflow with joy and thanksgiving for all he has done."

It's comforting to know that right now, today, God sees us in the light of His Son's perfection. He already sees us as we'll become when He calls us to Himself. He has put His stamp of approval on us already and He loves us as much today as He will ten years from now! This doesn't mean we can live indifferent lives. Out of love we want to work at becoming all He has purposed for us!

And that's about all for this week. Remember what Paul Tournier said, "He who does not go forward, goes backward." We're in a battle, but God is for us. Praise His Name!

Your sister in Christ,

Norma

10

Children —
To Have or
Have Not

10

⚜

Dear Norma,

I have been putting off writing for a few days because I have been a little bit down in the dumps, But today everything seems bright and cheerful again.

First of all, I'm not pregnant. To be truthful, I was a little bit sad, but I prayed before I went to see the doctor that no matter what the verdict was, it would be the Lord's will and I would be able to rejoice in it. And in a lot of ways another baby right now would mean big problems—so I'm glad. Still, babies *are* exciting!

The whole subject has made me think about birth control. I don't know what is right. I am unhappy with the IUD because I feel it is an abortive device, but I can't take pills yet as I am still nursing. I wonder if birth control is right for me at all. After all, the Lord has gone out of His way to make motherhood a smooth road for me. I always get pregnant quickly (the doctor calls me "Fertile Myrtle!"). Pregnancy, labor, and delivery have been easy and fun. My babies have been big, strong, and vigorous. Three weighed over nine pounds. None have any kind of health problem—not even an allergy. They seem to be above average in intelligence, too. My oldest daughter may skip a grade, and her younger sister in kindergarten can already read.

Many times I ask myself—why? What does God want? Bible verses like Psalm 127:3, "Children are a gift from God;" and even 1 Timothy 2:15, "So God sent pain and suffering to women when their children are born, but he will save their souls if they trust in him," have a great effect on me. I also believe that the Lord will not allow us to be tested above what we are able to bear. I would really like to know your opinion, Norma.

Can we trust the Lord to give us the "right" number of children and to provide for us? Or is it better to be responsible and limit your family's size to how many you can "afford"? Isn't that a little like making money your god, though? If children are really gifts from God, isn't birth control like saying, "No thanks, Lord" and superimposing our will over God's will?

I'm not questioning all birth control. It, too, can be one of God's blessings when rightfully used. But how do I know it is right for me? Couldn't this kind of trust be the best Christian witness my family could have? I really believe Psalm 37:25 is God's promise: "I have been young and now I am old. And in all my years I have never seen the Lord forsake a man who loves him; nor have I seen the children of the godly go hungry." I guess I'm pretty undecided and would appreciate your advice.

When it comes to my poor old house, I think it is beginning to shape up! Because I'm more interested in my home, my husband's more interested in fixing up around here. He started building shelves in the children's playroom six months ago. Now he's working on them again!

And speaking of shelves, I badly need them in several places around the house for storage. The other day my mother told me her company is getting rid of some metal shelves and they're only a dollar a shelf! So now I should become even more organized with a place for everything!

And I think I may be getting a vacuum cleaner soon! Sears has a very inexpensive canister model that would be fine for now and could be improved with the power-mate attachment later on. It's light-weight enough to carry up and down the stairs.

In my living room I have a couch and recliner that need to be reupholstered. Most slipcovers are expensive and don't last very long. Should I buy some material and cover them myself? Do you think it would work to staple a heavy material (like denim) over the back of the couch and then make cushion covers?

I have another problem—ants. Do you know how to get rid of them? We have them in the kitchen and bathroom. As soon as I got my crummiest cabinet all neat and orderly, ants started getting in it. Someone said bay leaf would keep them out, but it didn't. They aren't attracted by sweets. I'm in a dilemma and I hate to keep spraying poison.

Now that the girls are walking home from school, I have almost an extra hour to work in the afternoon and it's a blessing that the children can go outdoors to play. Last week the temperature was well into the seventies. We went to the park without coats and the baby slept on the grass! Of course, it doesn't stay nice too long. Monday night we went to bed during a terrible thunderstorm and woke up the next morning to four and a half inches of snow on the ground! But spring is definitely coming! Today is sunny and, as I was driving our five-year-old daughter to kinder-garten, our three-year-old piped up and said, ''Jesus give us this nice day, Mommy.''

I have finished reading your husband's book, *Manuel.*[5] It was very moving to me. I think you were blessed to raise your children in a missionary environment. I would imagine it helps them grow up not just believing in God, but as St. Paul says, ''rooted and grounded in faith.''

Sometimes I'm afraid for my children. I grew up in a Christian home but we never talked much about things involving deep emotions. I talk with my children, but often don't feel I'm getting through to them. Maybe I'm expecting too much too soon. They really are good kids!

5. Copyright © 1970 by Wycliffe Bible Translators, Inc., published by Fleming H. Revell Co.

I am praying for you and thanking the Lord for all you have done in my life. He has really given you the gift of encouragement.

In Christ's love,

Joyce

11

Do What is
Best For You

11

❦⊙❦

Dear Joyce,

I just returned from sitting in an out-patient waiting room for an hour and a half. I was to have a computer brain scan for this pain and pressure in the side of my head. However, due to a mix-up, I couldn't have it done today. I'm still undergoing tests but will let you know the results when they let me know.

It was good to get your letter today and I'm particularly happy you asked about birth control because I wanted to discuss this when I wrote about responsible living but didn't know whether I would be out of place.

I think what we need to do first is to separate *our* responsibility and *God's* total purpose for us. These actually come together at the point of choice, but they are still separate. To illustrate: God gives us food to sustain us, but just because the good gift of food is there, we shouldn't eat excessively. Food, while it sustains us, can also be hazardous to our health if we don't exercise self-control and choose to eat responsibly.

We know God is our strength and shield (Psalm 28:7), but to miss sleep five nights in a row because He is our strength, or walk blindfolded across a busy street because He is our shield, is irresponsible.

I believe God wants us to prayerfully seek His will for each choice we make which affects our lives and the lives of those around us. While children are a reward, heritage, and gift of God, should we haphazardly trust Him to give us the "right" number any more than we would trust Him to give protection across a busy street if we weren't making a responsible choice to look both ways and cross only when it was safe? The law of cause and effect touches every aspect of our lives! In connection with this, we need to ask ourselves, "What about illegitimate children? Are they gifts from God to those who choose this illicit union?"

Responsible effective Christian living, I believe, means prayerfully planning the number of children we feel we can adequately care for:

spiritually — time consuming, if we take Deuteronomy 6:7 seriously!
monetarily — education costs alone are staggering, not to mention clothing, medical and recreational needs.

emotionally -- filling the needs of each child with love, care, sensitivity, compassion and concern with time left over for our own emotional needs.

If my personality is such that I cannot be a good parent to more than one or two, perhaps it would be irresponsible to have more. If on the other hand I have the good gift of boundless energy, a carefree personality, and unlimited finances, I should still prayerfully plan my family, keeping in mind that the main reason for my existence is to "glorify God and bring Him pleasure" (Revelations 4:11; Colossians 1:16). I may not have financial worries, but can I still serve Him effectively if I'm bogged down with an overload of family concerns and problems?

Another good verse is 1 Corinthians 6:12: "I can do anything I want to if Christ has not said no, but some of these things aren't good for me. Even if I am allowed to do them, I'll refuse to if I think they might get such a grip on me that I can't easily stop when I want to." This passage goes on to tell us that our bodies are for the Lord. We are His temple. We are not our own; He is our rightful owner!

Seek His will with regard to your family size, taking into consideration your responsibility to God and those you would bring into this world. It's true, it's "lawful" for you to have as many children as you'd like, but perhaps it may not be "expedient!"

With regard to contraceptive devices, be sure to check with a reliable physician. If you feel that what you are presently using is harmful or unreliable, have your doctor prescribe what he feels is best adapted to you.

I feel I should also mention the Sympto-Thermal Method as described in Ingrid Trobisch's book *The Joy of Being a Woman*. Both you and your husband may find this the most helpful book you've ever read! Read her chapter entitled, "Living in Harmony with the Cycle," before deciding on a different contraceptive device than you're presently using. You may feel the Sympto-thermal Method is just what you've been looking for!

In the final analysis, it is not what I or others feel is right for you. After prayerfully seeking God's will and claiming His promised direction, you and your husband must do what you feel is best for you. Remember James 1:5: "If you want to know what God wants you to do, ask him, and he will gladly tell you, for he is always ready to give a bountiful supply of wisdom to all who ask him; he will not resent it." Keep in mind His best purposes for you (to glorify and bring Him pleasure), and then make your expedient (characterized by concern with what is suitable for you) choice.

Now back to your home! It's great you're getting those needed shelves and when you get the vacuum cleaner, it will revolutionize your cleaning!

Regarding the couch and recliner: slipcovers are not that easy! Through our local newspaper a couple of years ago, I ordered a book entitled, "Sewing for the Home." This gives excellent upholstering tips as I'm sure similar books on the market will do. After reading the instructions you will have a better idea whether you would want to tackle such a job or not. If you use a colorful blanket in the meantime, this may last longer than a throw and serve just as well.

About the ants: I had to smile when you asked me for advice. The reason? I began to realize again how nothing is wasted with the Lord. A few years ago we also had a trying time with ants. I never thought anything good would come from that experience, and now I'm able to share with you what we did about it!

First, I put several ant traps in the cabinets where they were the thickest. I also purchased a two-pound can of Vigoro's 10% Chlordane Dust and sprinkled this all around the outside of the house, right next to the foundation. I also sprinkled some by a back door entrance they were using to come in. Be careful that your small children don't get into it. I remember from my childhood that mother used to pour boiling water on ants and ant hills to get rid of them. This might work for you. Check in the yard for ant hills as it's best to get rid of them at the source. It will take a little time, but if you're persistent, they'll eventually disappear. I remember some days I was so upset I begged the Lord to take them away! Whether it was an answer to my prayers or the Chlordane—or both!—I don't know; but, praise the Lord, I finally won the battle and haven't had them since!

Now, before I close I do want to chat about a few leftover rooms, namely, bathrooms and closets.

The bathrooms definitely need a weekly cleaning. Use a sponge and one of the commercial cleaning agents to clean sinks, toilets, bathtubs and shower stalls. A long-handled brush is great for cleaning the inside of the toilet bowl. Sprinkle with cleaners, brush, and flush. Wipe down the tiles. If you have mildew on the tiles, save an old toothbrush and use it to get in those hard places, like the grout between the tiles. I've used cleansers, bleach, and ammonia products, but I still find it takes a lot of elbow grease!

If you have window cleaner, spray it on the mirrors and wipe dry with newsprint or paper towels. You can also clean by using wet newsprint or paper towels and wiping dry with fresh paper towels or newsprint. Use a disinfectant in the water to wash the floor. Wash the toilet seat cover and floor rugs periodically as needed.

Closets have a way of collecting clutter faster and easier than any room in the house. This is okay, but in order to keep organized, you will finally have to break down and clean them! If you're a saver, you can organize shelves in the closet with heavy corrugated boxes, keeping out only those things which are in current use. I like to separate summer and winter clothes. Keep clothes currently not in use in garment bags. Closet floors get dusty quickly and will need periodic vacuuming or cleaning.

Okay, let's take a typical "thorough" cleaning day. Don't try to use this day for cleaning the refrigerator or oven, doing a wash, or changing sheets. You'll have enough to do with cleaning, especially with your eight rooms! You can also space out a thorough cleaning over two days, or perhaps clean a room a day, if this fits better with your schedule.

You've been doing your daily PUAPA, so

today—your thorough cleaning day—you're going to first wash the dishes. There, that's out of the way! You've also checked the stove burner trays and washed these before you've "thrown out" the dishwater. The counters have been wiped clean and now, with a nice soft duster and cleaning product, wipe the refrigerator, stove top, hood, and oven. Dust the windowsills and check to see if the canisters, toaster or other counter-top items need to be wiped clean.

Sweep the floor. You have a kitchen table and chairs, so be sure to wipe these well (with a damp cloth if there's hardened food to remove). Move the chairs out of the kitchen to make floor scrubbing easier. Clean the floor with a wet mop, sponge, or rag, being careful to clean well in corners. An acrylic floor polish will last for months. However, with waxes there is a buildup which will eventually need to be stripped. Use one of the wax removers, following directions on the bottle.

Before dusting the living and dining rooms, pick up newspapers and remove to the basement or garage to save for a paper drive. Put other stray items where they belong. Be sure to dust windowsills, the front of the TV picture tube, furniture, pictures, knickknacks and, if needed, polish scratched furniture. Then vacuum. Or, in your case, sweep first, then dust.

You're doing fine! On to the bedrooms. Make the beds, hang up clothes, put toys, shoes, and other things in their proper places. Dust the tops of furniture, windowsills, pictures, headboards, etc. Vacuum.

Clean the bathrooms as described in this letter. Note closets or drawers that can be worked on during the week.

Vacuum the hall and stairs, sweep off the porches and, other than perhaps cleaning a fingerprinted door or wall, you're done!

We also haven't mentioned a good spring cleaning, when perhaps you take a solid week to shampoo rugs and furniture, and wash walls, curtains and windows. Some people like to do this once or twice a year. I've found doing these jobs as needed works better for me. Furniture polish on paneled walls or wood kitchen cabinets brings out a luster. A good product, specially for washing walls, makes it an easier task. Use one of the abrasive cleansers for crayon, pencil and other hard-to-remove marks, but don't scrub too hard as you'll take off the paint!

One final point. Your family is more important than your home, and you need to strike a balance. Strive to make your house homey and liveable rather than immaculate and sterile. It's not necessary to see your face in your floors and have everything in place at all times. Make it a nice place for *your* family. While you want your place to look nice for other people, your family's comfort comes first—not what will impress someone else!

That's about it for our "homemaking course." As I

said in the beginning, I'm not an authority, but I'm glad you've picked my brain! Until I hear from you, happy homemaking!

       Lovingly in Christ,

       Norma

12

⚜

Homemaking — An Art and Science

12

⚜

Dear Norma,

I'm still praying for you and I hope your tests all came out for the best. I hope you are feeling as good as ever. Psalm 16 is very comforting to me when I'm sick, especially verses 8 and 9: "I keep the Lord always before me; because he is at my right hand, I shall not be moved. Therefore my heart is glad, and my soul rejoices; my body also dwells secure" (*Revised Standard Version*).

Now, I am asking the same favor of you—please pray for my husband. He was riding his new motorcycle last Saturday when he fell off and broke his right collarbone in three places and fractured five ribs. We took him to the hospital and he came home on Monday. Today he is feeling much better but is still not able to move his right arm much without pain. He will be out of work for about three weeks.

You never knew when you challenged me to trustful living just how much of a challenge it would be! Or how comforting your words would be. I have reread that letter several times. And Norma, I want you to know, I have found God's grace to be sufficient!

Our Sunday morning worship at church was very reassuring to me. The very first hymn we sang was, "A Mighty Fortress is our God."

This accident represents a great financial setback for us. Our income is cut off and our medical bill has gone way up, but I do not feel worried. When I think about our money situation, all I feel is curiosity about how God plans to work things out for us!

Of course, I do hate to report that my battle with the housework took a turn for the worse this week. With so much to do for my husband and the children, I have been lucky to keep the dishes done! But, at least I know it is only a temporary situation and the first chance I get, I'll be back at work.

Thank you very much for sending me the poem you wrote. It seems to express a feeling which I have had. Your words touched me very much.

Last Wednesday when my daughters were at Midweek school, I visited with a friend. She shared with me two concerns that were on her mind. First, she has been having a terrible time keeping her house clean! And second, she is struggling with her Christian walk. We talked about how we could share our personal relationship with Jesus to our friends and other church members. Maybe a few of us can get together and light a fire under our congregation!

Don't you think the Lord could use us this way?

I have a few small bits of good news. First, I may be getting a washer and dryer soon! A friend is moving to a house that has a washer and dryer and will sell me her set for $80. The washer has a new motor! Laundry is a real problem since my husband's accident.

My baby is walking now! He'll be ten months old the nineteenth. It is so sweet to see him letting go and toddling off on his own. Of course, it's also rather sad to see my last little one growing up!

I've been trying to do some extra Bible studying lately and I see how helpful and important it is. I keep running into the phrase, ''God's steadfast love.'' I looked ''steadfast'' up in my dictionary and found it means firm, fixed, or constant. So you see, when God's world didn't live up to His expectations, He didn't give up on it and start over. He had steadfast love for His creation. He worked with it very patiently and brought about His plan for its perfection. Now I think I have to model myself after the Lord. When my plans for the house don't work out, I feel like abandoning the whole effort, but now I'm praying that Christ in me will help me to be steadfast and constant. Don't you think that if I work hard and patiently, with God's help, I can *redeem* my situation?

Since my husband is a carpenter, we could build a new house, but I am not ready for a new house. God really is ''guiding me with his eye.'' I'm very thankful.

I think the letters you've written to me would be helpful to lots of people. Housework is not highly valued. As a child I remember a neighbor who actually enjoyed housework. And I remember the women talking about her and saying she was a nut! But a Christian housewife can give glory to God in a special way. We want to—we just need someone to tell us how. There is so much involved in homemaking. It's not just a skill. It's an art and science!

Thank you for your advice about birth control. As of right now we both believe that four children are all we can afford. I always wanted seven children and find myself grieving over the children I won't have! I have to trust the Lord on this.

Please have a happy and blessed Easter. This Saturday we will be coloring eggs. My youngest daughter told me yesterday that she doesn't believe in the Easter bunny. "It's just somebody in a rabbit suit!" she said.

I'm hoping to visit a friend's church Wednesday. A Jewish Christian is presenting a service based on the traditions of Passover. And of course I'm looking forward to our own Easter morning celebration at our church.

Please take care and I will try to write real soon.

In Resurrection joy,

Joyce

13

A Vacuum Will
Make the Difference

13

Dear Norma,

I'm anxious to hear how you are and thought you might like to know that my husband is feeling much better. In fact, he's back at work already. He can't do the heavy work yet, but there is plenty to keep him busy. The doctor was surprised that his collarbone is healing so smoothly. The Lord is at work for us!

Thanks to you and the enormous help your letters have been, I can foresee the day when my housework will finally be under control! It's still a ways off, but I'm not discouraged. My housekeeping (or non-housekeeping) habits have been pretty well established in the eight years of my marriage and it is hard to break them. Getting used to new ways takes extra energy and concentration, too. Also, my family has to be retrained in lots of ways. But we are making progress and, with the Lord's help, it will be worth all the effort.

One benefit to me has been some important new insights into my own character. I know this is God's doing. I have learned that my lifelong habit of proscrastination is a real enemy. My mother always said, "If a job is worth doing, it is worth doing right." And since I seldom have time to do things "right," I just don't do them at all! I must keep reminding myself that God gives me *now* to accomplish whatever I can, not next Thursday or the day after tomorrow.

I've always felt that my best was just not good enough. Your advice has helped me to set more reasonable goals and more practical standards for myself so I'm not so easily discouraged.

Speaking of goals, I am trying to establish better housekeeping habits by committing myself to certain tasks. The first one is doing the dishes before bedtime. I have always left supper dishes until morning. I think having a neat kitchen to get up to in the morning will start the whole day off better.

I have also decided to devote one hour a day (8:30 to 9:30 a.m.) to housework. For that hour, the house has first priority. I take the phone off the hook and the children must find something to amuse themselves with for that time. No interruptions means I can concentrate and get much more accomplished. I also think it's good for the children to find their own entertainment. So far, though, all they do is follow me around! The baby especially needs to learn that he doesn't need Mommy 24 hours a day (only 23!). If I'm consistent, it may work out. After 9:30, I can bake cookies or go to the park and not feel guilty!

I want you to know that one of my friends came to visit this week and offered to help me clean house! We cleaned up the girl's bedroom and it really looks nice now. She said the same thing you have been saying, Norma, that a vacuum cleaner will make all the difference. I know the Lord will provide me with one. Anyway, since my friend is moving soon, we decided to exchange help. Once a week I will go to her house and help her pack and sort, and then she will come here and help me clean house!

And now I have something to share with you, that I haven't previously mentioned. I'm sort of writing a book myself! It is a collection of poems and parables that I wrote for my children to use as a morning devotion. If possible, I hope to have a few copies made to give to the other children on my Christmas list next December.

Here are two of the best. I know my writing skills are limited, but my three oldest children enjoy them!

Psalm 23
(paraphrase)

I am like a little lamb
That Jesus is always taking care of.
He shows me where the green grass grows
And takes me where the water is quiet
And good to drink.
He makes me feel happy
He shows me how to walk with him
And be like him.

Even if I go into a dark and lonely place
I will not be afraid

For you are with me, Jesus
And I know I'm safe with you.
You set the table for me
And make me feel important
You fill up my cup.

I am sure his love and kindness
Will be with me every day
And I will live in Jesus' house
Forever.

Mayfly
(Job 8:9)

Mayfly, mayfly
Life-in-a-day fly
Young in the morning
Old at night
We're all mayflies
In God's sight!

I wish that there was some way to repay you for all your kindness. I know the Lord will bless you, just as you are a blessing to other people. All my life I have repeated the Apostle's Creed and said, ''I believe in the communion of saints.'' I have learned from you a lot about the communion of saints. Thank you.

Love,

Your spiritual daughter and sister
in Christ,

Joyce

14

❦

You Don't Know
How Rich You Are

14

⁓◈⦚◈⦚

Dear Joyce,

I'm happy to report I'm almost my old self again.
Thank you for your prayers. I learned much through
this illness and recovery and will share some things
later. But first, let me answer your two good letters I
received the past couple of weeks.

I'm glad your husband healed quickly and is back
at work. And I'm happy you see evidence of God
working in your lives. He always is, but often, like
Peter, we get our eyes off Him and onto our
problems, and we begin to sink. I had to learn this
again these past few weeks!

I would certainly urge you to follow through and
get together with a small group to pray for your own
needs and the needs of your church. It only takes a
spark to light a fire! A good book to inspire you is,

What Happens When Women Pray by Evelyn Christenson with Viola Blake.⁶

I do hope you'll get that washer and dryer. I had hoped you'd have that vacuum by now, too. However, when you do get them, think what excitement you'll have!

Your remarks about God's steadfast love and relating them to your situation greatly blessed me. What a wonderful analogy! And I loved your two precious, fantastic poems!

Now, to share a few things I've learned through this illness. After what I first thought was an incorrect diagnosis and incorrect medication, I now see it was God's appointment for me. It wasn't pleasant. I have never been more frustrated or depressed, but looking back I see God in His tender love and care bringing me to the end of myself in order to teach me more of Himself.

I had begun to wonder where God was in all of this. It all seemed so senseless! I was resentful that I had to use my recent royalty check to pay the hundreds of dollars on tests I never needed in the first place. Then I began to resent never having enough money for anything and having to live out of the "missionary barrel." I began to complain I hated feeling like a charity case all the time, and because I felt this way, I also experienced feeling indebted to all those who had given to us over the years.

Revelation 12:10 tells us that Satan is the accuser (or faultfinder) of the brethren. But he doesn't help

6. Copyright 1976, Victor Books, Wheaton, Ill.

us see *our* faults. That's what the Holy Spirit does when He guides us into all truth (John 16:13). Rather, Satan kept me blinded to my own failings by helping me find fault with others and my situation.

Ephesians 4:1 in *J. B. Phillips'* translation says, "Accept life with humility and patience, making allowances for one another because you love one another. Make it your aim to be one in the Spirit, and you will inevitably be at peace with one another."

Satan, on the other hand, says, "Poor you! You're so hard done by. Go on! Demand your rights. You shouldn't have to live like this. You don't have to take it lying down. Fight for what's rightfully yours, After all, you deserve it."

After our Sunday School class a couple of weeks ago a gal I hardly know (I think I've only spoken to her once), handed me an envelope. I opened it before the church service and burst into tears when I read the following:

Dear Norma,

It is my understanding that you and Hugh would both benefit greatly if you were able to attend an important Wycliffe conference in Mexico next month. I also understand you might not be able to make this trip with Hugh unless extra funds become available to help with the expense.

This may seem strange, coming from someone you don't really know that well. I'm sure you understand much better than I do, how the Lord works in mysterious ways, but I happen to have some extra money coming to me at this time. I believe it is my responsibility and privilege to give a portion to God's work. I know that you and Hugh are very special servants of God, and I would like to have this small part in supporting your efforts to serve the Lord.

Please accept this gift from God through me.

Wow! In my discouragement I began to wonder if God knew about all the money we were using on medical bills, and then He "zaps" me with this! It was as if He said, "Look, my child, of course I know about your medical bills and other needs. Just to let you know everything is under my control, I'm giving you a *want*. Don't you have that money I allowed you to have from the sale of your book? Use it. Cease from your worries. I will supply all your need just as I've promised."

With this encouragement, I phoned my friend, Phyllis Gettig, and shared with her God's goodness. I also shared how I had let myself get to the point of hating to be a "receiver" all the time and how a couple of bad experiences from "givers" in our twenty-one years as missionaries had tarnished the joy I should have had over God's provision.

"Don't you realize what a blessing you and your family are to us?" said Phyllis, when I finally let her get a word in. "Besides, we have to have someone to give to! When you tell us how the Lord has provided in all these miraculous ways, we all rejoice with you and our faith is strengthened. You don't know just how rich you are!"

Her one comment, "We have to have someone to

give to," helped me more than she'll ever know. I began to see that our whole life-style is God-appointed—not just our involvement as part of the Wycliffe team. I got down on my knees and told the Lord how sorry I was for all my stubbornness and struggling instead of resting in Him and accepting life.

I was reminded of Paul's statement, in Philippians 4:11, where he stated that he had learned to be content when things were difficult or prosperous. I now see it isn't a lack of success or lack of God's provision if we never seem to get ahead by the world's standards. It's learning to accept and be obedient to Him in His appointed place. But more than that, if we can bring Him glory in our present life-style so that others can be blessed, what a privilege!

If all this isn't enough, another "good" has resulted. I quit my work at the bookstore. While I've thoroughly enjoyed this outlet and ministry, I realize I don't need the extra stress. Hugh has enough for me to do with the editing and typing I do for him. I keep thinking I need some other "ministry," but the Lord has made it clear that for now my ministry is through the help I give my husband and the many letters I write each month.

I'm sure you can see how my seemingly depressing situation the past few weeks has turned into something glorious. And I'm not through yet! I've thought a lot about my role as a woman. I've found it hard to understand women who are forever striving for an identity of their own and realize now that I've been doing the same thing! But the Lord has slowed me down enough to see that as I accept myself and my responsibilities as wife and mother and live in harmony with His will for my life, I enjoy my uniqueness as a woman. I'm happier with me as is my family. This is true freedom! I am free to be me when I know and understand God's purposes for me.

In one of my first letters I mentioned two qualities Paul, in Ephesians 5, exhorts women to put into practice—submission to and reverence for her husband. But the Scriptures also have more to say about the ideal woman. Namely, King Lemuel's remarks in Proverbs 31:10-31.

The amazing thing is that his wise sayings were taught to him by his mother! We would do well to pass on this wisdom to our own children.

1. Her husband can trust her. (Remember our meaning of *trust?* He can rest his mind in his wife's integrity.)
2. She will richly satisfy his needs.
3. She will not hinder him or do him evil (hold back, oppose, frustrate, inhibit, smother).
4. She will do him good (be of benefit, be a blessing, be of service, be an improvement for him, or as Genesis 2:18 says, "a companion for him, a helper suited to his needs").
5. Willingly keeps occupied.
6. Prepares creative meals.
7. She gets up early to get breakfast for everyone and plans what she'll do that day.
8. She looks for ways to add to their income.

9. She's energetic—a hard worker, watches for bargains (stretches the budget), gets all her work done.
10. She looks for ways to help others.
11. She thinks ahead and plans for her family's needs.
12. She not only makes beautiful clothes for herself, but she sews and makes things for her home.
13. She doesn't slander, belittle, or attack her husband's personhood. (How else could he be so well thought of?)
14. She makes things for others.
15. Even when she's going through rough times, her strength and dignity show through.
16. She's not afraid of old age.
17. Her words are wise and kind.
18. She's interested in each family member and all their activities.
19. She's never lazy.
20. Her children think she's great, and her husband is always saying, "You're the best thing that's ever happened to me!"
21. She takes God seriously.

The last point should be the first! For only as we take God seriously (through prayer, Bible study, meditation, and worship), will we be successful in all He has given us to do.

My husband, Hugh, in his book, *They Dared to be*

Different,[7] closes with the hero expressing, "Because I take God seriously, I am in the process of succeeding." I guess that's what these letters have been all about—success through effective Christian living—in our lives, our homes, and in our community.

In my little book, *What Kids Katch from Parents*, it was my wish to get across one point—the importance of daily living out the reality of Christ in our lives. In these letters, while sharing a few practical homemaking hints, my goal has been much the same. I believe that as I put Christ first, or take God seriously, He will do as He's promised and "add all these things unto me." Wisdom to live my life pleasing to Him, wisdom to bring up my children to know and love Him, and wisdom to be a great wife and homemaker! Note, I didn't say, "housekeeper." Many women rebel because they no longer want to be the "housekeeper" for their families. If that's all they are, I don't blame them! The dictionary says that a *housekeeper* is a female who looks after a person's household. In other words, a domestic. And you can hire someone to do that! A *homemaker*, on the other hand, is a *manager* of a household, as a *wife* and *mother*. It's a great calling, but then we have a great God!

7. Copyright © 1976 Harvest House Publishers, Irvine, Ca. 92714.

God bless you for letting me share these random thoughts with you. You've also blessed me with your letters and good insights.

Learning to live pleasing to Him,

Norma

15

❦

Next Year
I'll Be Free!

15

Dear Norma,

I hope you are completely recovered now and feeling fine. I'm still remembering you in my prayers. My husband's injuries have healed and he is riding his motorcycle again. I am praising the Lord (for the healing, not the motorcycle!). I had a little free time so I thought I'd give you a progress report.

My house is looking so much better! My living room is in pretty good shape. Last week I cleared out all the clutter and cleaned the air conditioner and TV. Our television sits on top of an old console TV which doesn't work. I covered the old TV with a tablecloth and now it looks like a table—much neater.

A friend gave me an old wicker chair. The back and seat are covered with red corduroy, the same as my living room curtains. I put a nice colored blanket over the recliner, so it looks better. The whole room is really improved. I would like to find a cover for my old seven-foot couch. And I think the room needs some greenery—a few hanging plants.

On Saturday we invited my folks over for supper! It really was great because Mom has been working too hard lately and she really seemed to enjoy something different. I made a simple meal of beef stew, salad and homemade bread, with brownies and ice cream for dessert. We ate at the dining room table which I had covered with a nice lace tablecloth (church rummage sale—$1.00).

You can tell I'm making some progress. I count every little step forward as a victory for the Lord. He encourages me. Of course, for every two steps forward, I take one step back. But I try to think of every setback as temporary and not get discouraged.

My own attitude is one of the hardest things to change. There are times when I ask myself if I really want things so nice and neat after all. It was all so familiar and comfortable when it was messy! I know this is wrong, but new life-styles don't come easy.

It isn't easy for my family either. My daughters are beginning to rebel at Mom's continuous chorus of "put it where it belongs." Hopefully, their bad habits are not as deeply ingrained as mine; and if we work together, we can soon establish some good, new habits.

My three-year-old is my delight. He goes around saying, "Dis pace all messy. Us have to keep it up!" Today he came to me talking about " Sugar Hill." I asked him where it was and he pointed up. Since the children had just been playing in the upstairs bedroom, I thought he meant upstairs. But he said no. I asked my daughter what he was talking about and she said, "Oh, he means heaven." "Yes," he said, "I say 'Sugar Hill'!" I haven't any idea where he got it, but it seems like a pretty good three-year-old description of heaven to me! When I questioned him some more about it, he said, "It is ten blocks away and you go there and Jesus gives you presents!" I think I like his theology!

The girls are finishing up this year's school. Next year I'll feel so free! No one in afternoon kindergarten!

I am now the proud owner of a third-hand washer and dryer. It is so great to do my wash at home. I am hoping I can get a clothesline set up outdoors so I can hang my wash up to dry this summer.

I painted the bathroom this week. It isn't quite finished yet, but what a difference! It has always been a bright sea-green with turquoise self-adhesive paper around the tub (awful!). Now it is white. Much better. I've always hated that room, and now I kind of like it!

I'll never be an interior decorator, but I'm improving the looks of things around here. I'm trying to figure a way to hang guitars on the wall. This will kill two birds with one stone—fill a large empty wall and make a place to keep the guitars!

I'm still struggling to improve my housekeeping skills. It is hard, but there is progress—the Lord is guiding me with his eye!

In your last letter you told me about how you had been blessed even by your illness. What you said about Satan as the faultfinder really hit home for me. I think self-pity is one of my pet sins. I was whining to the Lord because a girl I was trying to strike up a relationship with, hurt my feelings. You showed me that my own attitude was the most hurtful thing.

I can't thank you enough for all your thoughtfulness and good advice. Please take good care of yourself and return to good health.

In joy and peace,

Joyce

16

❦

Goose Bumps
in My Stomach

16

There were other notes and letters that Joyce and I exchanged and we'll continue to. I was especially happy to tell her that my going to Mexico resulted in a neurosurgeon correctly diagnosing my ear-head problem. It turned out to be my mandibular joint. Apparently I should have been seeing my dentist! The last thing the specialist had said to me, before going to Mexico, was that he thought it was a tumor in the ear. I felt the trip to Mexico was more than an opportunity to attend the Wycliffe conference. It was as if the Lord wanted to put my mind at ease, that nothing was "growing," and then through the prayers of many of my friends He healed me. After two visits to the dentist, he said the problem was getting better on its own!

I was especially delighted when Joyce wrote to tell me she had been asked by the Christian Women's

Club in her area to lead a Bible study. There were the old feelings of inadequacy and apprehension; but to me it was amazing how, in such a short time, she had been open to growth and change.

Somehow, I found myself feeling that there was still one final progress report to be made. I had a strong urge to talk to Joyce personally instead of through our usual letters.

After finding her phone number through the kind efforts of telephone operators, I said, "Hello, Joyce. This is Norma. Norma Steven."

"Oh!" said Joyce in an excited voice. "Oh, yeah, hi!"

"Well, hello," I said in an equally excited voice.

"I'm surprised!" she said. And then we both laughed together. I made a comment about having goose bumps in my stomach myself (and then I wonder why my children come out with strange remarks?).

I explained my reason for calling, and asked how things were going.

"Great!" she said. "I have a letter in the mail telling you all the good news."

"I thought I should be hearing soon," I said, "but I wanted the fun of hearing your voice."

"And I'm glad to hear yours," she said. Then she excitedly told me she was finally able to get a vacuum. "I love it!" she said. "It's my best friend!"

We talked about the Bible study, which was to begin in two days, and shared what had been happening in our own lives since we last wrote; and then I said, "I hope the Lord lets us meet some day."

"So do I," she said. "And thanks for everything."

Two days later Joyce's letter arrived and my family and I rejoiced together at the great things God had done in her and her family's life in just eight months since we first began to write.

" 'Well,' she began, 'we can both praise the Lord. Yeah! I got a vacuum cleaner! Just last week. And is it ever a little wonder! It was on sale and my husband told me to get it. It's just what I've needed. I really don't get to use it as much as I'd like because the baby follows me around chewing on the cord, playing with all the attachments, trying to 'help' me!

"I am feeling so much better about the house and about everything in general. I have been thinking about last January when I was finally able to get out of the house after being snowbound for two days. I went to the grocery store and happened to see your book, *What Kids Katch from Parents*, on the book rack. I took it home and read it straight through. Then I wrote to you and you threw me a lifeline! With so much help from you and the Lord, I'm finally on top of things.

"Of course, not everything is perfect or even close. There are lots to do, but now I have this feeling that I can do it! The house is not immaculate but I can handle it. I'm on top of the situation and able to jump in and tackle the mess when I need to.

"Today I began cleaning my biggest problem room. It's a small room off the kitchen where we keep our freezer and my sewing machine, and tons of old junk. It's the worst place in the house and I've hated to even think about trying to sort it all out. But today I got a good start on it. The rest can be done a bit at a time. I hope I can make it sort of my prayer closet, too.

"After I finished the work, I was reading a booklet on prayer and came across the verse from Revelations 5:8 where it refers to 'golden vials filled with incense—the prayers of God's people.' The book pointed out that this means God is a saver. He's keeping all our prayers!

"A big part of my housekeeping trouble comes from my reluctance to part with the past. I'm always trying to save things that will enable me to hang on to the past. But if God is saving all the important parts of my history, I can toss out most of my silly, earthly momentos! I guess I just discovered I don't need all that excess baggage!

"So much new, good stuff is going on in my life right now. I wish I could tell you about all of it, but I'm almost too busy to write long letters!

"First of all, I am meeting lots of new people here. I'm going to be the Brownie Scout leader for the first and second grade girls. My assistant leader is a Christian! She has two children the same age as mine. We have a lot in common. I think we may end up real good friends!

"With regard to my Bible study, I hope to have around ten in the class. It will be on Thursday evenings from 7:30 to 9:00 in our Town Hall. The topic is prayer. I'm a little scared to be starting to lead other people and would sure be grateful if you would remember me in your prayers.

"Since my mother is working for a while in New York City, my sister and I decided to give her house a 'thorough' cleaning. Guess where I started? Kitchen cabinets! I'm really enjoying making everything neat and tidy.

"I'm making a throw for my couch. I found some perfect material (for 99 cents a yard). I think my living room is starting to look kind of cozy and warm!

"Tomorrow is the first day of school for my daughters. They are so exicted they could hardly get to sleep. I think both will have good teachers this year. I am looking forward to the regularity of the school schedule. It means we will be having big family breakfasts together and the day will be off to a good start. Also I hope, with only two boys at home, my housekeeping chores will be easier!

"I must brag a little bit, Norma. I've been playing tennis a lot this summer and I've lost ten pounds! I weigh 125 pounds and have lots of energy and feel good.

"I'm having a problem with my attitude towards the baby. I'm regretting his growing up so much. I realize I'm sometimes soft with him and don't insist on reasonable behavior from him. But I pray a lot for wisdom to see and correct my mistakes. I believe it would be sinful and selfish of me to coddle him and not give him a good foundation for his life. He is really sort of hard to handle anyway because he is so quick and active. Strangers are always joking when they see him and say he should be tied up! He is extremely well-coordinated and an accomplished climber. His grandparents and father don't even like baby-sitting because he has to be watched so closely! Many times I've wondered how the Lord works everything out so perfectly to the smallest detail. I have a need to lavish attention on this baby and he has needs that require a lot of my attention!

"I'm still reading through your letters regularly—for inspiration as much as for information!

"Thanks again for your prayers, especially for my vacuum cleaner. It sure is a useful thing, makes my life easier, too!

Much love,

Joyce"

Epilogue — Steps to "Greatness"

"Okay, Lord. So Joyce seems to have found the answer, and has been able to turn the corner in her life toward becoming a better homemaker. But what about me? You know I have good intentions, but one day just seems to lapse into another, and before long the house utters one final sigh and settles down into a portrait of seemingly total neglect.

"I don't even have Joyce's excuses, if you can call the lack of a vacuum, washer or dryer good reasons for not being able to keep a clean house.

"Lord, I really want to be your woman. So, please, is there some way you can show me, too, how to become a beautiful woman—inside and out—who is able to care for her home as you would like?"

Homemaking does indeed offer each woman an opportunity to achieve greatness—in the eyes of God and in the eyes of her family. Each woman comes into marriage with a different set of qualifications, determined by her personality, abilities, and growing up experiences; but, there are several steps which each one of us must take, regardless of background, in order to become the great homemakers God would have us be.

In review, what are some of these "handles" to grab hold of, to succeed in our God-given role as a homemaker?

1. *Know where you stand with God.* We are all sinners. Romans 3:23 reminds us that "all have sinned; all fall short of God's glorious ideal . . ." We must be able to acknowledge that fact, and then receive God's free gift of salvation through belief in His Son, who loved us so much that He died for us. Having asked God to forgive our sins, we next must accept His forgiveness. In doing so, we can only then forgive ourselves, and thus accept ourselves.

God didn't ask us to clean up all the bad habits of our lives, and then come to Him, asking to be His child. No. He asks us to bring to Him the broken, fragmented pieces of our lives, and He will cleanse us and make us whole persons again, starting from within.

2. *Set aside time, each day, to spend with God.* Ever awakened in the morning, with that sickening thud in your stomach as you realized that today is the "tomorrow" you were dreading yesterday? You just want to turn over, pull the blankets firmly up over your head, and block out reality.

If so, you may well have an attitude problem—approaching the day already defeated.

Tomorrow, when the alarm sounds, try this: Quote to yourself the well-known verse from Psalms, "This is the day which the Lord hath made; I will rejoice and be glad in it." Ask the Lord to be the Lord of your life, today. Don't dwell on past failures, or (for that matter) on past glories, and don't concern yourself, needlessly, about tomorrow.

Jesus assured us that our heavenly Father will meet our every need, if we give Him first place in our lives and live as He wants us to: "So don't be anxious about tomorrow. God will take care of your tomorrow too. Live one day at a time" (Matthew 6:34).

Find a time alone with God, to seek out His wisdom for the day. To know the Father, we need to keep the channels of communication open between Him and us through prayer and by reading His Word.

The time or place may vary, according to our schedules, and we can be assured that we'll never *find* time. We just have to *take* the opportunity, and daily seek God and His plan for our lives.

3. Remember that *God is not a God of confusion—but of order.* Paul tells us, in 1 Corinthians 14:33 KJV: "For God is not the author of confusion, but of peace . . ." Or, as *The Living Bible* says, "God is not one who likes things to be disorderly and upset."

Strike a soar spot?

Then, don't miss this exciting news! God has given us His Spirit to instruct us, and teach us His ways. "Strange as it seems, we Christians actually do have within us a portion of the very mind of Christ" (1Corinthians 2:16).

God is eager to help us bring peace and order to our lives. He wants to help us.

4. *Set priorities.* Just as God desires to teach us to be good stewards of our material possessions, He wants us to be worthy stewards of our time and our talents. Many a well-meaning mother has far overextended herself as she became involved in the PTA, local Girl Scout council, missionary aid society, and Wednesday night choir rehearsals. All of these ventures are *good* activities, but the vital question to be answered is this: Am I involved in too many "good" activities, and therefore missing God's very "best" for my life?

During the course of a week's time, check yourself on these questions:

Am I spending a portion of my time with God?

Does He really have first place in my life?

Have my spouse and I set aside any special time just for ourselves?

Have I truly listened to the conversations of my children? Am I aware of their spiritual and emotional needs as well as their obvious physical needs? And, am I meeting these needs?

When we cut through the superficiality of our activities, and focus in upon what God would have us do with our time, we can begin to see certain activities as high priority; others, as mere busyness.

5. Having set priorities, now follow through. Make a plan—*set some goals*—and work the plan. That's the name of the game! Determine what your priorities, as a homemaker, are—and carry through with your plan. The perfect schedule for one woman, will not work for another. We are all different, displaying varying amounts of incentive, motivation and energy. So determine the plan that works best for you, and hang in there!

We have discovered that there is much more to homemaking than just "housekeeping," tidying and cleaning our place of residence. When our children are grown, and leave our home, what will their memories be? Will they remember an aseptic, sterile environment, where they could never relax for a moment for fear of spoiling the newly polished floor or shampooed rug? Or, will they cherish memories of laughter, and times of relaxation when—sprawled on pillows on the living room floor—they have played and laughed and cried together as a family?

As we seek to live each day of our lives as responsible homemakers, knowing that we are held accountable to God, we will discover the meaning—via direct experience—of the adjectives: frugal, creative, disciplined, responsible and trustful. And we will discover, also, the sweet feeling of contentment as we blossom in our newly defined and refined role as "homemaker."

"Charm can be deceptive and beauty doesn't last," says Proverbs 31:30, "but a woman who fears and reverences God shall be greatly praised."

Glorify God in your everyday behavior, no matter how mundane the task, and you will find yourself in the shoes of the wife whose "children stand and bless her; [and] so does her husband" (Proverbs 31:28).